LOOK IT UP
Now in a fully revised edition

1. You and Your Body
2. People and Customs
3. What People Do
4. The Prehistoric World
5. Ships and Boats
6. People of Long Ago
7. The Sea
8. The Earth
9. Cold-Blooded Animals
10. Warm-Blooded Animals
11. Sport and Entertainment
12. The World of Machines
13. Land Travel
14. Flying
15. Outer Space
16. Index

Photo Credits: All-Sport; Alfa Romeo (Gt. Britain) Ltd; Austin Rover Group Ltd; Bedford Commercial Vehicles; British Tourist Authority; Canadian Pacific; Citroën; Colorsport; Godfrey Davis Europcar Ltd; Douglas Dickins F.R.P.S.; Mary Evans; Fiore; Ford Motor Co. Ltd.; Robert Harding; J.M.Jarvis; JCB Sales Ltd; LAT; London Transport; J.G.Mason; National Coal Board; National Motor Museum; Peter Newark's Western Americana; Novosti; Picturepoint Ltd; Paul Popper; SAAB (Gt. Britain) Ltd.; S.N.C.F.; Swiss National Tourist Office; Union Pacific; VAG (UK) Ltd.; ZEFA.

Front cover: Camerapix Hutchison Library.

Illustrations: Jim Bamber; Eddie Brockwell; Robert Burns; Dick Eastland; Dan Escott; Bryan Evans; Elizabeth Graham-Yool; Colin Hawkins; Richard Hook; Eric Jewell; Roger Phillips; Mike Roffe; Barry Salter; Michael Whelply.

First edition © Macmillan Publishers Limited, 1980
Reprinted in 1981, 1982, 1983 and 1984
Second edition © Macmillan Publishers Limited, 1985

All rights reserved. No reproduction, copy or transmission of this publication in any form or by any means, may be made without written permission

Chief Educational Adviser
Lynda Snowdon

Teacher Advisory Panel
Helen Craddock, John Enticknap, Arthur Razzell

Editorial Board
Jan Burgess, Rosemary Canter, Philip M. Clark, Beatrice Phillpotts, Sue Seddon, Philip Steele

Picture Researchers
Caroline Adams, Anne Marie Ehrlich, Gayle Hayter, Ethel Hurwicz, Pat Hodgson, Stella Martin, Frances Middlestorb

Designer
Keith Faulkner

Contributors and consultants
John E. Allen, Neil Ardley, Sue Becklake, Robert Burton, Barry Cox, Jacqueline Dineen, David J. Fletcher, Plantagenet Somerset Fry, Bill Gunston, Robin Kerrod, Mark Lambert, Anne Millard, Kaye Orten, Ian Ridpath, Peter Stephens, Nigel Swann, Aubrey Tulley, Tom Williamson, Thomas Wright

Published by Macmillan Children's Books
a division of Macmillan Publishers Limited
4 Little Essex Street, London WC2R 3LF
Associated companies throughout the world

ISBN 0 333 39731 2 (volume 13)
ISBN 0 333 39568 9 (complete set)

Printed in Hong Kong

Land Travel

Second Edition
LOOK IT UP

Contents

	Page
THE HISTORY OF LAND TRAVEL	**4**
Early travel	6
Carts, wagons and stagecoaches	8
TWO WHEELERS	**10**
Early bicycles	10
Motorcycles	12
CARS	**14**
Early cars	16
Early motoring	18
Special vehicles	20
Racing cars	22
Land speed records	24
VANS AND TRUCKS	**26**
Heavy goods vehicles	28
Heavy loads	30
BUSES	**32**
Early buses	34
Coaches	36

	Page
ROADS	**38**
Early roads	38
Motorways	40
Bridges	42
Tunnels	44
RAIL	**46**
Passenger trains	46
Freight trains	48
Locomotives	50
Special railways	52
Early railways	54
Signalling	56
CITY TRANSPORT	**58**
Underground railways	58
Trams	60
Taxis	62
DID YOU KNOW?	**64**
INDEX	

THE HISTORY OF LAND TRAVEL

These pictures show how land travel has changed. At first people carried loads on poles. They rolled heavy loads over logs. Then men cut slices of log to make wheels. This made land travel much easier. Carts were made for animals to pull. Now we travel by bicycle, car, bus and train.

carrying loads on poles

pack animals

wagon

carriages

steam engine

truck

modern car

motorcycle

racing bicycle

electric locomotive

streamlined locomotive

rolling stones over logs

Roman wagon

early bus

Penny-Farthing

early car

early steam train

charabanc

safety bicycle

Model T Ford

steam train

high-speed train

Early travel

Long before wheels were invented people rode on animals. They used animals to carry goods too. First the animals had to be tamed. Then bundles or baskets could be loaded on their backs.

In some countries animals are still used to carry goods and people.

Camels can travel in the desert. They have wide, padded feet. They can carry heavy loads without sinking in the soft sand.

Reindeer pull sledges over soft snow in Lapland. Several reindeer may be used to pull a heavy load.

Llamas are used by people in hilly parts of South America. They can walk safely on rough and steep mountain tracks.

Horses, donkeys and mules can travel on bad roads carrying heavy loads. They are shod with iron shoes.

Elephants can carry goods and people. Have you ever ridden an elephant at the zoo?

Carts, wagons and stagecoaches

No one knows who invented the wheel, but it was a great discovery. It made travelling much easier. The first wheels were solid wood. They were heavy. Gradually men learned how to make light, strong wheels.

The Romans used wooden wagons pulled by horses. The wheels had spokes.

This Indian bullock cart has simple solid wheels. Wheels like these were invented about 7,000 years ago.

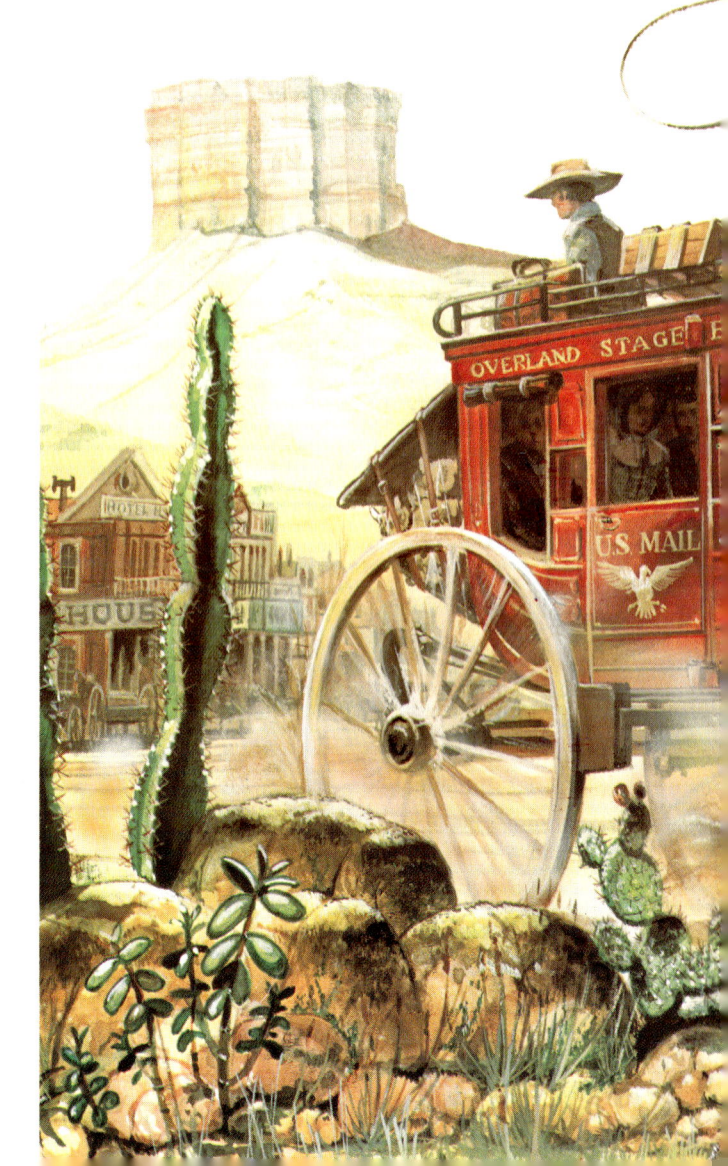

Long ago there were no railways and roads were poor. People travelled from town to town by stagecoach. It took all day to travel 100 kilometres. The coach was pulled by a team of horses. People travelled in stagecoaches like this one about 100 years ago. They crossed the American continent. Some stagecoaches also carried the mail.

CALIFORNIA STAGE CO.

OFFICE, ORLEANS HOTEL,
SECOND STREET, BETWEEN J AND K,
SACRAMENTO.

J. BIRCH, - - - PRESIDENT.

DAILY CONCORD COACHES
Leave the Orleans Hotel, Sacramento, carrying the U. S. Mail, viz:

Marysville and Shasta,
Touching at
Charley's Rancho, Bidwell's Rancho, Hamilton City, Oak Grove, Clear Creek, Lawson's, Tehama, Campbell's Rancho, Red Bluffs, Cotton Wood Creek, One Horse Town, Middletown, Covertsburg, Shasta, Yreka and Pitt River Diggings.

Posters like this one displayed travel times and fares.

TWO WHEELERS

Early bicycles

The first bicycles did not have pedals. Riders sat astride a wooden beam. They pushed against the ground with their feet. Later a metal tube was used for the framework of the bicycle and pedals were added. Early bicycles had wooden wheels.

The Hobby Horse was a bicycle without pedals. It was popular 150 years ago in Britain and France.

cycling 90 years ago

The Penny-Farthing bicycle was popular 100 years ago. It was difficult to ride and uncomfortable.

Cycling was very popular 90 years ago. People enjoyed riding in the countryside.

Motorcycles

The first motorcycles were made more than a hundred years ago. In France Pierre Micheaux fitted a steam engine to his bicycle. A few years later Gottlieb Daimler made a small petrol engine. He used this engine to power his bicycle. People found that it was cheap to travel by motorcycle.

Daimler designed and made the first motorcycle. A small engine drove the back wheel. This machine showed how engines could be used.

Motorcycles with side cars used to be popular for family travel. Most of them are now used as racing machines like the one below.

The Japanese are the most famous makers of motorcycles. This is one of their powerful motorcycles above. They make smaller machines too.

Special motorcycles are made for young children to ride. A six year old girl is riding the one opposite.

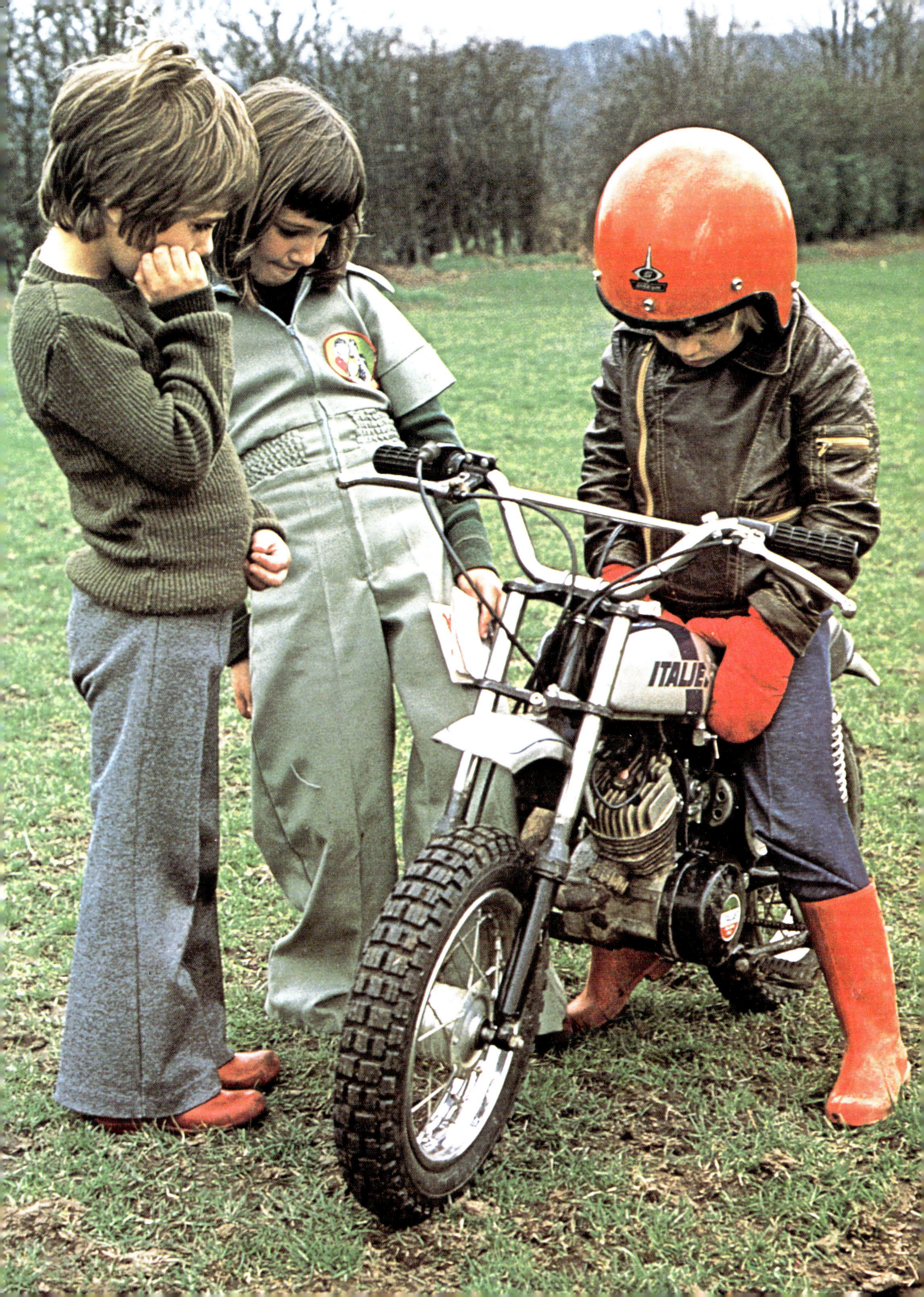
ITALJE

Metro (Great Britain)

Mercury (USA)

Citroën (France)

CARS

Cars are made in many parts of the world. Many countries sell their own cars. Some countries sell cars made in other countries too.

These are just a few of the cars that are made. Follow the lines. They show you where on the map each car comes from.

Alfa Romeo (Italy)

14

Saab (Sweden)

Toyota (Japan)

Audi (West Germany)

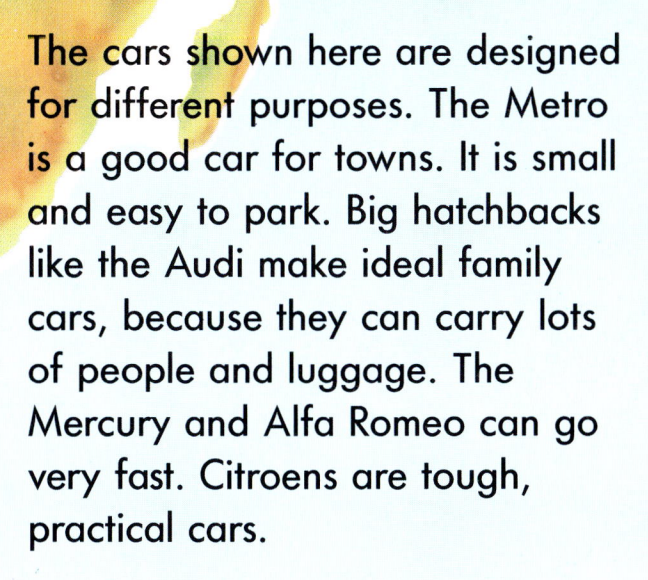

The cars shown here are designed for different purposes. The Metro is a good car for towns. It is small and easy to park. Big hatchbacks like the Audi make ideal family cars, because they can carry lots of people and luggage. The Mercury and Alfa Romeo can go very fast. Citroens are tough, practical cars.

Early cars

Many of the first cars looked rather like wagons or small carriages. Each one was powered by an engine instead of a horse. Other early cars looked like big bicycles. They too had an engine. The wheels were often made of wood, with solid rubber tyres. It must have been cold driving in the winter.

early car

The most successful early cars were made about 100 years ago. They were designed and built in Germany by engineers. Karl Benz made three-wheeled cars like the one below.

This old four-wheeled car is a Stanley. It was driven by steam.

1885 Benz

1870 tricycle

16

1903 Daimler

This car was made by Gottlieb Daimler. Petrol engines were better than steam. They could start up faster.

carriage

1903 Oldsmobile

Early motoring

The first cars were built for wealthy customers. Motoring was very expensive. The first speed limit in British towns was seven kilometres an hour. At first people and animals were frightened of cars. They were not used to the noise. The cars seemed so big and powerful.

1919 Model T Ford

This is a 1919 Model T Ford. About 15 million of these cars were mass produced in 20 years.

By 1926 cars were cheaper to make. More families could afford to buy them. Three companies, Austin, Ford and Morris, made cheap cars. The car on the right is an early Austin.

Special vehicles

Have you ever tried riding a bicycle over a muddy field or over sand? It is very difficult. Cars and trucks get stuck in mud and snow. It is not easy to get them out. Special vehicles are made to travel over difficult ground. Some are used to help us. The machine on the right helps harvest fruit.

Earth movers help build roads and railways. They have big wheels and can dig and push the earth.

The beach buggy is designed for use on the sand. It has a small powerful engine and is fun to drive. Sand has to be kept out of the engine.

The skidoo is a working vehicle. It is used by explorers for travelling over the snow. Some people work at weather stations in the Arctic. They use skidoos too.

Racing cars

The first motor race took place in 1899. The cars raced from Paris to Rouen. The most famous type of car racing is called Grand Prix. In this picture you can see racing cars on a Grand Prix circuit about 50 years ago.

Go-carts are mini racing cars. They often have a top speed of about 60 kilometres an hour. Go-carting is a sport which is great fun.

Rally driving is a sport that is fast growing in popularity. One of the most famous rallies is the East African Safari. The drivers have to cross very rough ground.

23

Land speed records

A Frenchman named Rigolly held the land speed record at the end of the last century. He drove an electric car at 96 kilometres an hour. The record is now over ten times faster.

Thrust 2

The world land record is held by Englishman Richard Noble. His car is called Thrust 2. It averaged 1019 kilometres an hour. Its engine was taken from an old fighter plane.

The Blue Flame was a rocket-powered vehicle. It was used to break the land speed record in 1970. Gary Gabelich drove the Blue Flame at 1014 kilometres an hour.

VANS AND TRUCKS

There are many different kinds of vans and trucks. All of them are built to do certain jobs. Some are made to carry heavy loads. Others bring us special help when we need it. What jobs do these vehicles do?

mini bus

tanker

delivery van

refrigerated goods lorry

fire engine

goods truck
car transporter
caterpillar transporter
dump truck
road sweeper
ambulance
dustcart
bus
builder's lorry
Land Rover

27

Heavy goods vehicles

Most heavy goods vehicles are in two parts. The engine and the driver's cab form one unit. This is joined to a trailer. Heavy loads are carried on the trailer. When one trailer is unloaded the engine can be used to pull another trailer. On the right you can see an articulated truck in New York.

articulated truck

heavy goods vehicle

28

This trailer is a tank with wheels. It carries liquids safely. Some trailers carry containers.

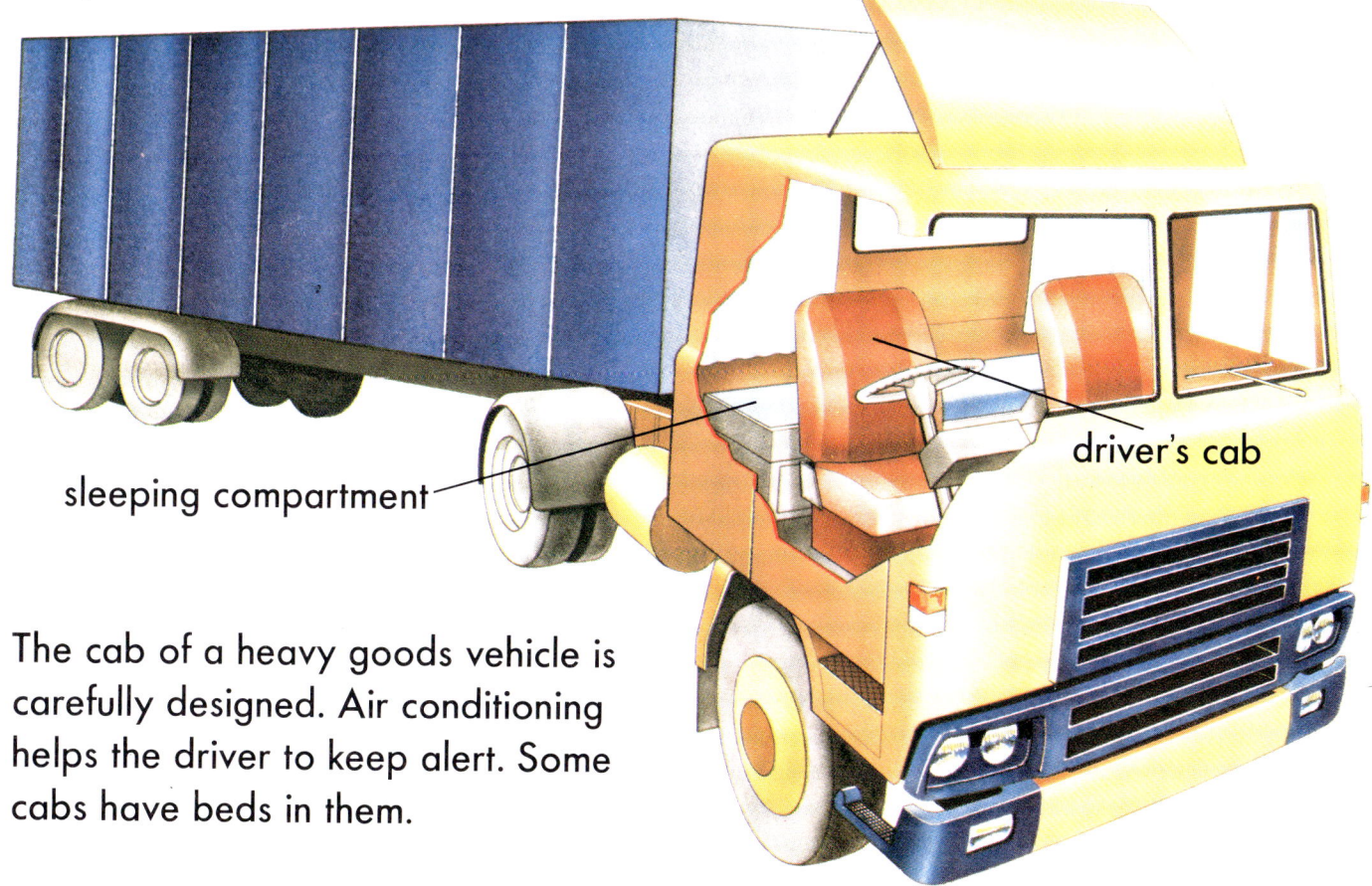

sleeping compartment

driver's cab

The cab of a heavy goods vehicle is carefully designed. Air conditioning helps the driver to keep alert. Some cabs have beds in them.

Heavy loads

Sometimes very heavy loads have to be moved by road. Special low loaders and transporters are used. The Space Shuttle on the right weighs 68 tonnes. It is carried on a low loader so that the load is spread over a large number of wheels. It has a special escort because it is so big.

This heavy earth-moving machine can only travel very slowly along the ground. A low loader can carry it quickly from place to place.

This is a car transporter. The cars are carried on two levels. The driver can deliver seven cars at a time.

Space Shuttle

BUSES

There are buses in nearly every country in the world. They are made in all sizes and shapes. Some are double deckers, like the London bus below. In many places there are open-top buses. The passengers get a good view as they travel along. On the right you can see a bus travelling in Afghanistan.

These West African people are boarding a bus in Sierra Leone. All their belongings are on the roof.

Early buses

Today town buses are big. They can carry as many as 80 people. The first buses were much smaller. Some were driven by steam engines. Others were pulled by horses.

The first London bus service was started over 150 years ago by George Shillibeer.

This was the first bus service in France. People could ride on top of the bus. The driver sat at the front and drove the horses.

steam coach

The first steam coach service was started about the same time as the first bus service. A steam engine pulled along a coach.

Fifty years ago there was no roof on the top deck of any London bus. It was a long time before roofs were added.

1923 London bus

Coaches

Travelling by motor coach is faster and more comfortable than going by bus. It is cheaper than travelling by train. Ships and car ferries can carry coaches. On the left you can see a coach leaving a ferry.

Below you can see a Greyhound coach. These coaches travel from coast to coast in North America.

Many people spend their holidays on coach tours. They stay in hotels and travel from place to place by coach. With their big windows and high seats, coaches are ideal for sightseeing tours.

Seventy years ago families enjoyed trips in coaches like this. They were known as charabancs, and were used for outings.

37

ROADS

Early roads

The Romans built thousands of kilometres of very straight roads. They used flat stones.

The surface of this road is covered with rounded stones, called cobble stones. Many old cities and towns in Europe have cobbled streets. They are very slippery and dangerous in wet or icy weather.

Most roads were just muddy tracks 500 years ago. Carts and wagons often got stuck.

About 200 years ago better roads were built. People paid a toll at the turnpike gate so they could use them. The money paid for the new roads.

turnpike

39

Motorways

This is a modern motorway. The idea of motorways started in Germany over 50 years ago. Walking and parking along the motorway are not allowed. The vehicles travel at high speeds. There are no crossroads except at different levels.

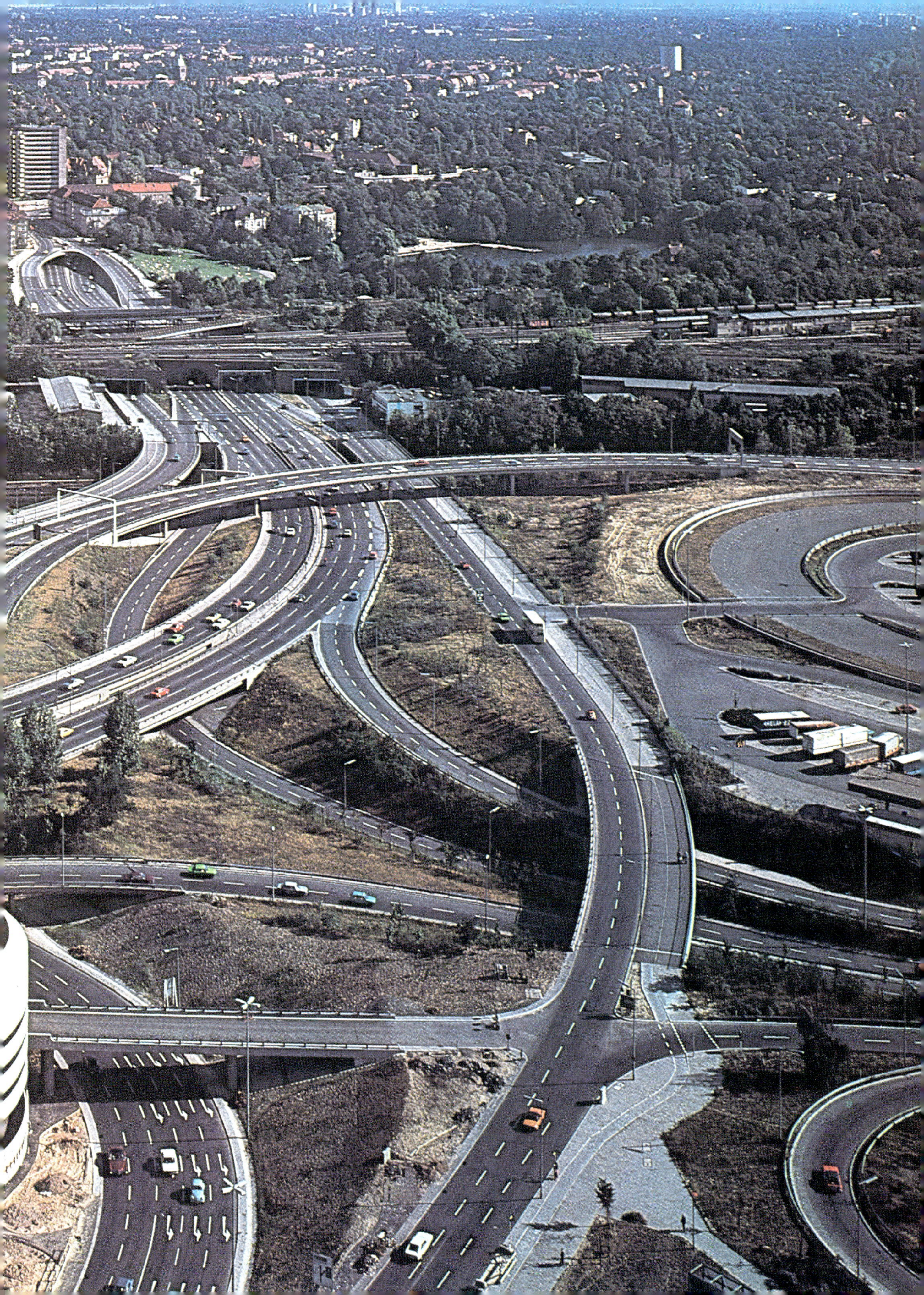

Bridges

Bridges are used by pedestrians, cars and trains. Without them, journeys would take much longer. There are three main kinds of bridge. They are called the beam, the arch and the suspension bridge.

This is a long beam bridge that crosses a lake. A number of beam bridges have been joined together. The model below is a beam bridge.

This is an arch bridge. The arch holds up the roadway. Some arches are made of stone or concrete. This one is made of steel.

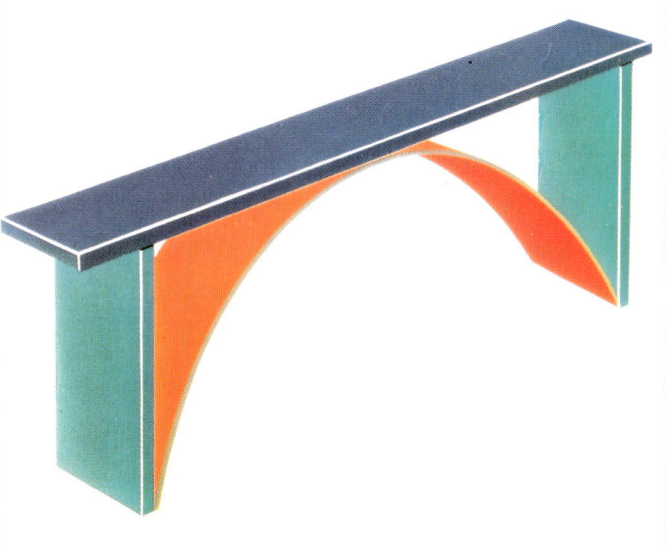

You can make a beam bridge with bricks and beams of wood. Keep the beams short. What happens if you walk over a long beam?

Make an arch bridge with cardboard. Make another without the arch. What happens if you put a large stone on each bridge?

42

A viaduct is a bridge. It has a number of very tall arches joined together. Trains go over viaducts, to cross deep valleys.

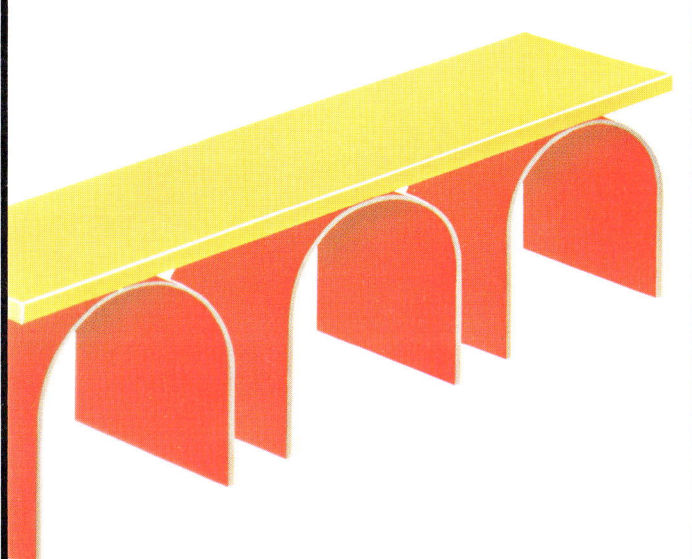

Try making a model viaduct. Use stiff paper. Is this bridge as strong as your model of the single arch bridge or the beam bridge?

This is a suspension bridge. The road is suspended from steel cables. The Humber suspension bridge is 1500 metres long.

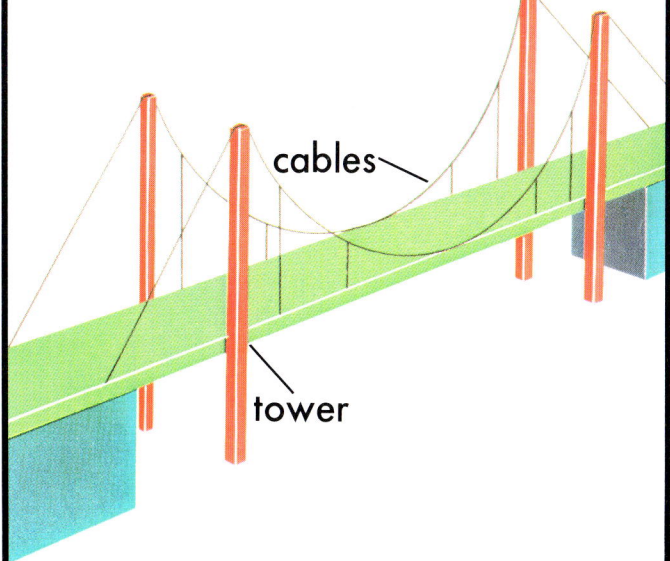

cables

tower

The weight of the suspension bridge rests on the two towers. The steel cables are fixed very firmly into the bank at each end.

Tunnels

Tunnels are made to take roads through hills. They are also built for railways. The Mont Blanc road tunnel is 11 kilometres long. It goes from France to Italy through the mountains. It was cut through solid rock. Explosives were used to blast the rock.

When a tunnel is built through clay or soft earth a metal framework is used. This is called a shield. A tunnel lining is built behind the shield. This lining holds up the roof.

This worker is blasting a ventilation shaft for a tunnel. Holes are drilled into the rock. Men pack explosive charges into them. The explosives are fired electrically.

dirty

poisonous fumes

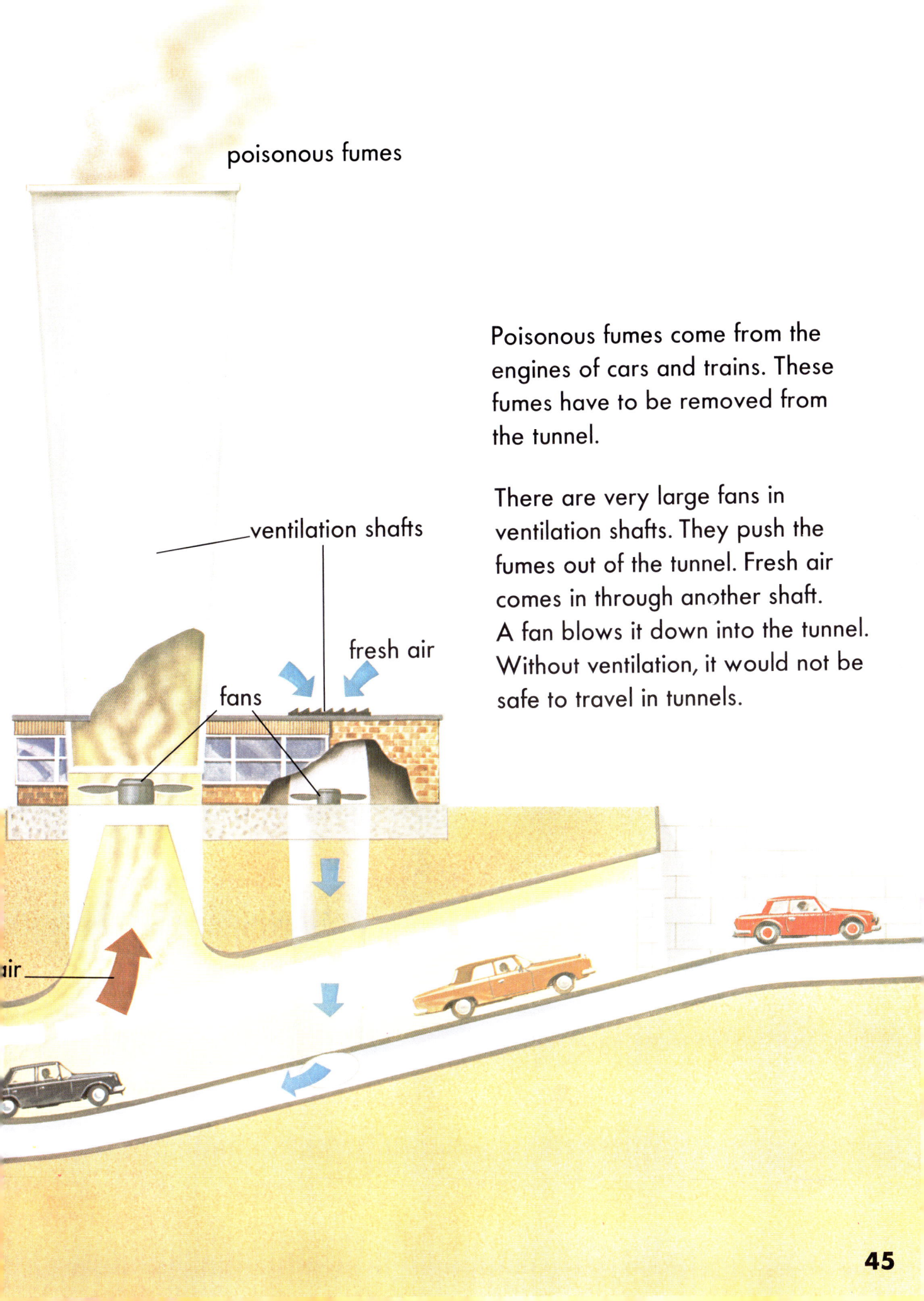

ventilation shafts

fresh air

fans

air

Poisonous fumes come from the engines of cars and trains. These fumes have to be removed from the tunnel.

There are very large fans in ventilation shafts. They push the fumes out of the tunnel. Fresh air comes in through another shaft. A fan blows it down into the tunnel. Without ventilation, it would not be safe to travel in tunnels.

RAIL

Passenger trains

Every day millions of people travel by train. Modern trains are as comfortable as most cars. They are also much safer. Stations are busy places. The station in the small picture is Hamburg. On many trains you can eat in a dining or buffet car.

an old dining car

On the right you can see a diesel train in England.

The world is slowly becoming short of oil and petrol. In time more and more people will travel by train. On many railways there are double-decker trains. A train like this saves hundreds of car journeys.

French double decker train

Freight trains

The first railways were built to carry coal and other heavy goods. Trains which carry goods are called freight trains. Special car transporters are used to collect new cars from car factories. Some people like to drive their own car on holiday. They take their car with them by train.

car train

Sometimes one locomotive is used to pull many large wagons. This is a freight train travelling through Canada.

Many goods are transported in containers. They are easy to load and unload because they are all the same size. This container depot is in West Germany.

49

Locomotives

At first all railway engines were steam powered. Steam trains crossed America, Australia and Europe. In China and India steam trains are still used. Now diesel and electric locomotives are used in most countries. These trains cost less to run and can travel faster.

Electric trains do not have to carry their fuel. Power comes from electric cables overhead.

This is an Indian steam locomotive. Burning coal or wood makes the water boil in the engine. This makes steam which drives the wheels.

In Britain the 'Intercity-125' train is powered by two diesel engines. Diesel engines burn oil.

51

Special railways

The first railways were built to help men who worked in mines and quarries. Some special purpose railways are still used. The railway on the right is in a coal mine. It takes miners to the coal face. On very steep mountains cable cars are used. It is sometimes too difficult to build a mountain railway.

cable car

This mountain railway has a toothed rack between the rails. A toothed wheel fits into this to help the train climb steep hills.

Early railways

Puffing Billy was built in 1813. It is one of the oldest steam locomotives in the world. You can see it on the right. William Hedley built it at a coal mine in Newcastle, England. Puffing Billy pulled coal wagons from the pit to the River Tyne for 50 years Today you can see it in a museum in London.

The first steam train to run in Germany was called The Eagle. It is on the left.

The engine below is called Tom Thumb. This engine took part in a race with a horse. The horse won. But the American railway company decided to buy locomotives.

54

The first railway for passengers was opened in 1830. It ran from Manchester to Liverpool. There was a competition to find the best engine. Robert Stephenson's engine, The Rocket won the prize.

Signalmen with flags gave the first train drivers their signals.

Years later signalmen in a signal box worked the signals mechanically.

Nowadays automatic lights are used as signals. The trains move over switches which work the signals.

Signalling

Railway signals are as important as trains or tracks. The safety of passengers depends on a good signalling system. In a modern signal box there is a plan of the track. Moving lights on the plan show the positions of the trains. The men in the signal box control the trains on many kilometres of track.

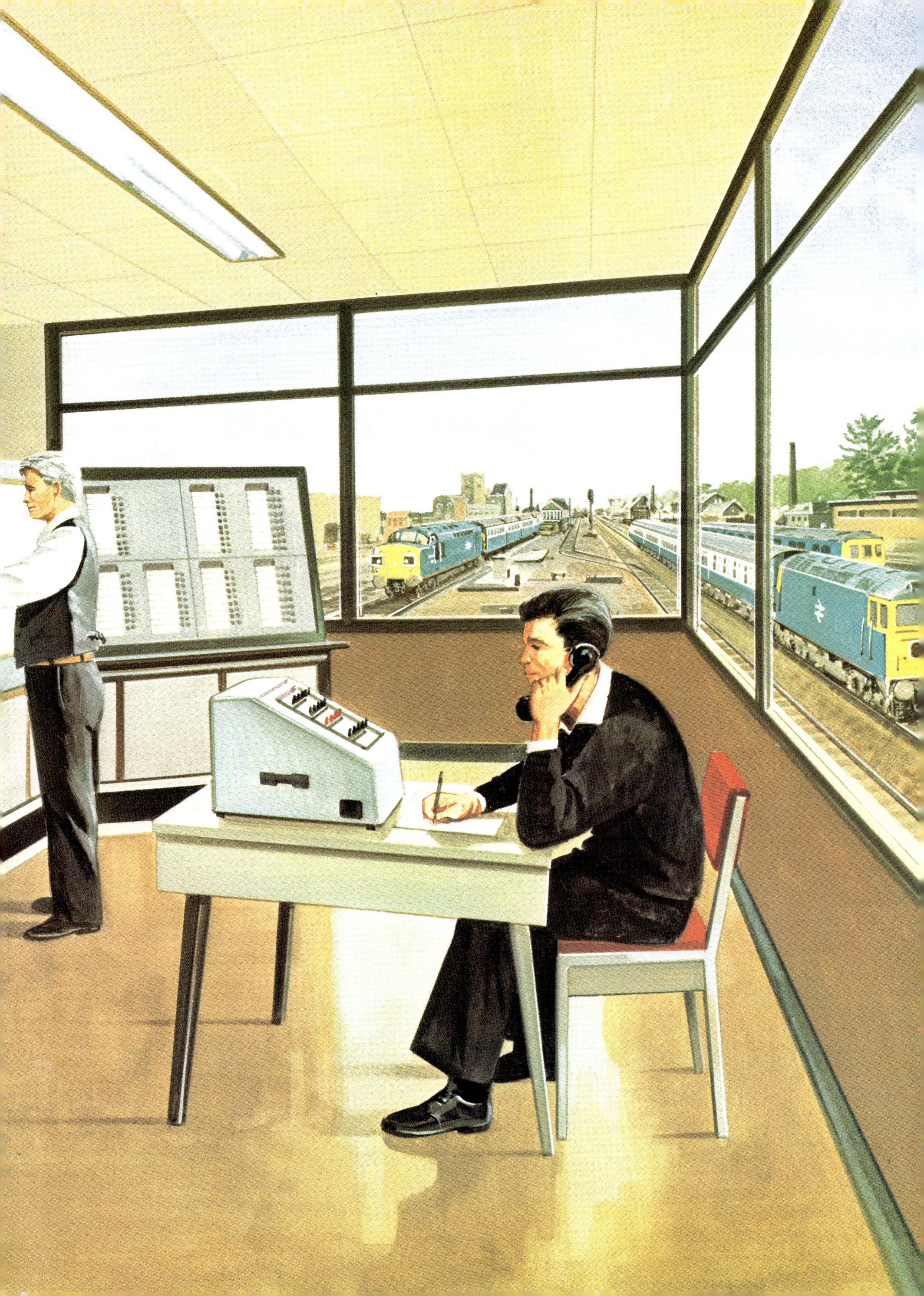

CITY TRANSPORT

Underground railways

Underground railways are a quick and easy way of travelling. Many cities have underground trains. This station is in Moscow.

London was the first city to have an underground railway. The first tunnel was built over 100 years ago. The picture on the right shows how the underground tunnels link up. The picture below shows men building the new Jubilee Line.

entrance

transit tunnel (northbound)

ticket hall

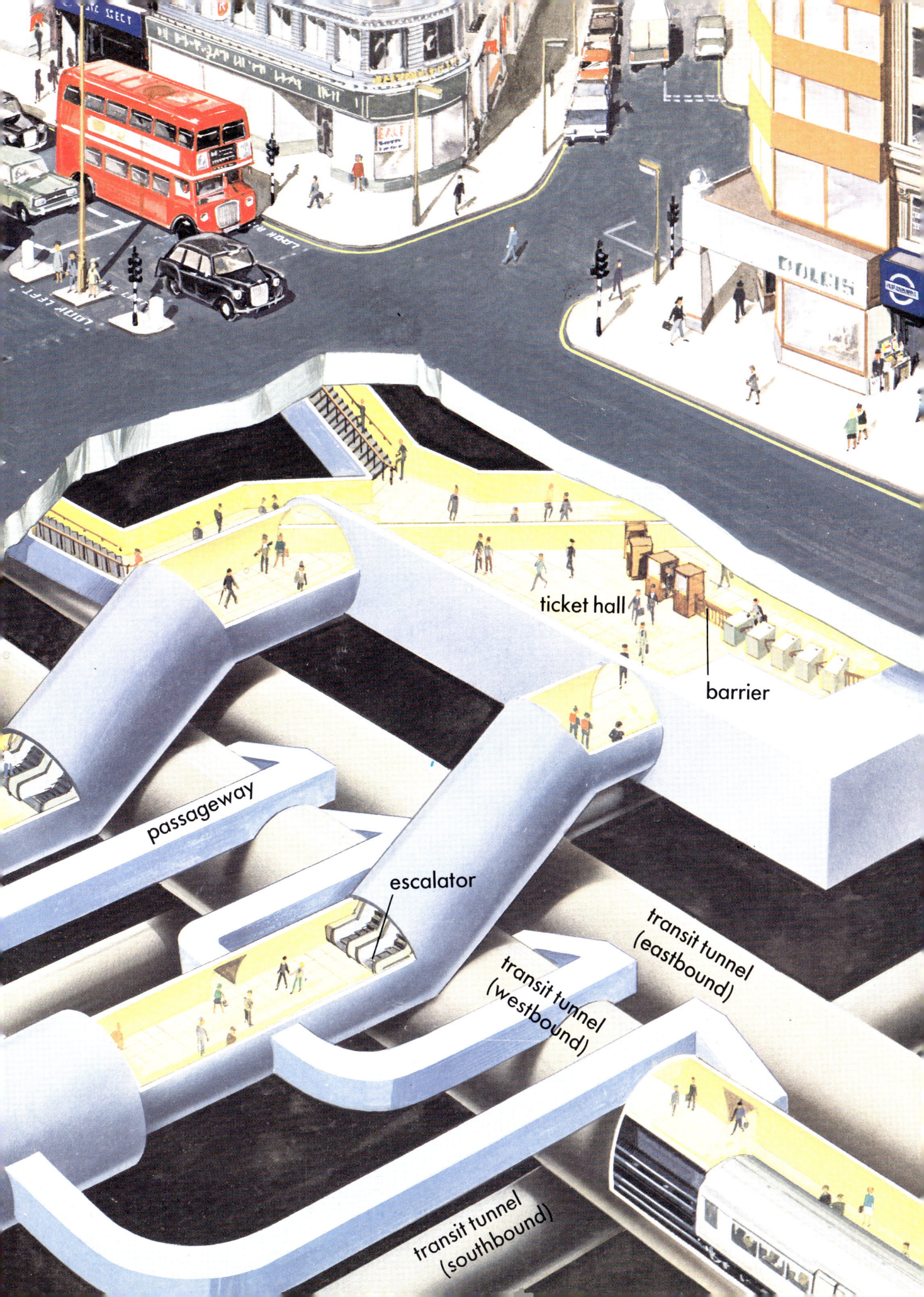

barrier

passageway

escalator

transit tunnel (eastbound)

transit tunnel (westbound)

transit tunnel (southbound)

Trams

Trams run along tracks on the road. Sixty years ago there were trams in many cities. Some were pulled by horses. Others were steam powered. Most of them were powered by electricity from overhead cables. There are still trams in some cities today.

This tram in San Francisco carries people up steep hills.

The steam tram on the left is used in India. It can burn coal or wood. It provides cheap travel for many people.

Today there are only a few tramways left. Most have been replaced by buses and cars.

The modern tramway in the picture above runs through the streets of Melbourne in Australia. The wires at the back of the tram connect with the electric cables overhead.

A trolley bus is a mixture of a bus and a tram. It is electrically powered. It does not run on tracks.

Taxis

One of the quickest ways to travel in a busy city is by taxi. You tell the driver where you want to go. He drives you there with your luggage. Motor taxis have meters. These record the cost of the journey as the taxi moves along. This is very helpful to the passengers. They know how much they must pay the driver.

This is a Chinese rickshaw. The driver pushes his passenger. Some rickshaws are pulled by bicycle.

In New York there are yellow taxis called cabs.

Most London taxi cabs are black. Their shape is different from other cars. They are designed to turn easily in narrow streets. London taxi drivers have to take an examination all about London streets. If they pass they get a licence to drive a taxi.

DID YOU KNOW?

A family of badgers was living by a small road in England. Then men came along to build a motorway. They thought the motorway would be dangerous for the badgers. So the men built an underpass especially for the badgers.

There are more new cars than babies in America each year.

In 1769 Cugnot built the first kind of car. People had never seen anything like it. They thought he was mad and put him in prison.

INDEX

Animals   6-7
Articulated trucks   28
Beach buggies   21
Bicycles   10-11
Bridges   42-43
Bullock carts   8
Buses   32-35
Cable cars   52
Cars   14-19
Car transporters   30-31
Carts   8-9
Charabanc   5, 37
Coaches   36-37
Cobbled streets   38
Cycling   10-11
Diesel trains   47
Double deckers   32
Early travel   4-11, 18-19, 38-39
Early vehicles   34-35, 54-55
Earth movers   20, 30
Electric trains   50
Freight trains   48-49
Go-carts   23
Grand Prix   22-23
Greyhound coaches   36-37
Heavy goods vehicles   28-29
Heavy loads   30-31
Hobby Horses   10
Horses   7-9
Intercity-125   51
Jubilee Line   58-59
Locomotives   50-51

London Underground   58-59
Model T Ford   19
Motorcycles   12-13
Motorways   40-41
Mountain railways   53
Passenger trains   46-47
Penny Farthings   11
Racing cars   22-23
Railways   46-61
Rallies   23
Rickshaws   62
Roads   38-41
Roman roads   38
Side cars   12
Signalling   56-57
Skidoo   21
Space Shuttle   30-31
Special vehicles   20-21, 52-53
Stagecoaches   8-9
Stanley steam cars   16
Steam coaches   35
Steam engines   50-51
Subways   58-59
Taxis   62-63
Trailers   28-29
Trams   60-61
Trucks   26-27
Turnpikes   39
Two wheelers   10-13
Vans   26-27
Wagons   8-9
Wheels   8-9